IRREVERENT DICTIONARY
OF
INFORMATION POLITICS

BY

PAUL A. STRASSMANN & JOHN KLOSSNER

The Information Economics Press • New Canaan, Connecticut

Text and Composition: Paul A. Strassmann
Illustrations: John Klossner, Klossner Studies
Printing: Edwards Brothers, Lillington, North Carolina

For bookstore or bulk purchases, please contact:

PEER-TO-PEER COMMUNICATIONS, POB 640218, San Jose, CA 95164-0218
Phone orders (800) 420-2677, (408) 435-2677; Fax (408) 435-0895

For single copy purchases, please contact:

THE INFORMATION ECONOMICS PRESS, POB 264, New Canaan, CT 06840-0264 New Canaan, Connecticut 06840-0264
Phone orders (800) 800-0448; Fax (203) 966-5506

Printed in the United States of America
2 3 4 5 6 7 8 9 10

Strassmann, Paul A. and Klossner, John
   1. Politics   2. Information Technology
   3. Business Management   I. Title
   1995   658.4
Library of Congress Catalog Card Number: 94-74275
ISBN 0-9620413-5-1

INTRODUCTION

One of the many complaints about computer people is their propensity to express themselves using too much jargon. For that reason, most books about computers include a glossary to explain what should have been said in plain English.

Paul Strassmann's latest book *The Politics of Information Management* (The Information Economics Press, 1995) includes a glossary to make information politics more understandable. It lists terms you may have heard elsewhere, but wondered what they really signify in the context of organizational disputes. Therefore, his explanations are political, not technical.

Reviewers labeled the glossary "irreverent." One reviewer called it "hysterical, being worthy alone the price of a scholarly book." Most early readers kept clamoring for additional witty illustrations from John Klossner, who produced forty cartoons for the *Politics* book. There was also a demand for a collection of Paul's one-liners that could be understood in less than five minutes should a reader wish to avoid spending hours pouring through more than five hundred pages of his text. What you see here is much that many information managers may wish to see or hear about information politics.

This dictionary defines Quality as something that can be judged only by the customers, not the authors. In the spirit of the marketplace, we decided to satisfy the wishes of our customers. We hope you enjoy it.

Paul A. Strassmann, New Canaan, Connecticut
John Klossner, Cambridge, Massachusetts

Index to Illustrations

Index to Illustrations

"Computerization is the conduct of management
by other means."

ಀ

"A little humor makes computerization more
human."

Acquiring **C**omputer **L**iteracy: Playing games while appearing to work.

Application: An accumulation of features from long departed users. Discarded when the complexity becomes incomprehensible, even though it works.

Artificial **Intelligence:** The expensive automation of tasks previously done cheaply with judgment.

Auditors: Experts in guessing the menu by examining the leftovers.

Authentication: The need to verify who is sending an electronic message.

Awards for Excellence in Computing: Media beauty contests judged on self-reported claims. Earned by the PR department, not the CIO.

Budget Cut: A tourniquet around the neck to stop bleeding from the foot.

Business Planning: Documentation of how computer technology will be blamed in case of failure.

Business Process Redesign: A process for increasing cooperation in the workplace.

Business Reengineering Consultant: A cannibal who will invite you to a dinner party.

II

Buzzword: A new word for old solutions that masquerade as the answer to current problems. Repackaging old buzzwords is what advertising departments do for vendors and consultants.

Career Self-Destruction: When the followers think they are the leaders. A common aberration among financial and systems analysts.

Centralization vs. Decentralization Contests: Boxing matches at budget time.

CIO: Chief Information Officer. An executive who tries to manage what others consider to be their privileges.

Command, **C**ontrol & **I**ntelligence: Acquiring electronic equipment to solve military problems encountered in prior wars.

© 1995 by The Information Economics Press

Computer Budget: A bag of cash big enough to buy dinner where the menu and the number of guests are unknown.

Computer Literacy: Converting managers, engineers, and scientists to typists. Turning secretaries and all hired help into computer experts.

Concept of Operations: An explanation of goals and principles that can be acted on by operating personnel. An ingredient missing from consulting and government committee reports.

Configuration Management: Trying to make the components from different vendors work together.

Consensus Estimating: A method for estimating the benefits of computerization that claims to be a science.

Consolidation: Legitimized hijacking of the budget of one organization by another. Winners get the biggest toys.

Consultants: Contractors who learn what your own people could have learned given the same time and money.

Convergence of Media: Replacing the telephone, television, radio, record player, and videotape with a microcomputer.

Data: Raw material of the information age. Useful only after prolonged digestion. The output keeps the bureaucrats employed.

Decentralization: The redistribution of the central computer budget to where it is no longer traceable.

Defenestration: A way to dispose of losers in palace revolutions in old Central Europe. Also known as "voluntary resignation" in contemporary U.S.

Development Tool: Any software technique that a programmer is accustomed to using. Usually a hard-to-follow trick to assure indispensability.

Digital **Equipment Corporation:** An organization that forgot that smaller fish can eat bigger fish.

Displaced Attention: Cutting the computer budget as a way to cope with a sinking business situation.

Downsizing Through Amputation: An approach to reducing staff. Assumes that severing limbs is the only way to become healthy and profitable.

Downsizing Through Weight-Loss: An approach to reducing staff. Assumes that fasting is the only way to become beautiful.

Electronic Data Interchange: A technique for getting rid of facsimile transmissions.

E-Mail: A message distribution method that works only for the self-selected.

Employees: Your most important asset, as stated in the annual report. An easily liquidated resource, as reported in the news.

Employee Relations: Avoidance of criticism in case it might be construed as unfair discrimination.

Encryption: A method for making text illegible to unauthorized readers. Guarantees privacy for citizens as well as criminals.

Enemies: Erstwhile friends who keep reminding you what you did wrong.

Espionage: Interviewing a competitor's systems personnel on the pretense of potential employment.

Evolution of the Human Species: A theory as interpreted by computer people.

Executive: A person who may be relied on to make wise, intelligent, and strategically prudent decisions after having first tried other possibilities.

Expert Systems: Complex logical metaphors that shift the blame for misjudgments to computers.

Facsimile: A backward technology that remains immensely popular because everyone knows how to use it.

Floppy Disk: A 3.5 inch square piece of paper, plastic, and metal through which you can lose all your information assets or get them poisoned.

44

Goals: What is desirable, but not always practical.

Governance: Rules that balance acceptable conduct and risk.

Government Regulations: A franchise for lawyers to assist in dealing with government rules.

Hierarchical Design: A finance officer's concept of an ideal system.

IBM: A management who wrote the classics but did not study barbarians.

Implementation: The really tough job that follows after visions, goals, principles, and plans are announced. Usually delegated to those who had nothing to do with formulating those visions, goals, principles, and plans.

Incentives: A reward for overcoming keyboard phobia, such as keeping your job.

Infoassassination: A crime that leaves no fingerprints.

Information: Something understood by the originator, but not necessarily by the recipient.

Information Baron: A bureaucrat who knows that power is control over information.

Information Conflict: A euphemism for bureaucratic confrontations.

Information Hermit: Someone who finds it easier to communicate with a personal computer than with family, customers, fellow workers, and bosses.

Information Highway: Resembles a toll road insofar it may become a new a scheme for collecting taxes.

Information Implosion: Collapse of an organization because the decision makers talked only to themselves.

Information **P**olitics: Recognizing that good intelligence makes it easier to win.

Information Security: The ratio of capabilities of infoassassins vs. infodefenders. Currently, infodefenders are out-numbered and underpowered.

Information **Spoofing:** When the enemy makes you believe his misleading messages.

Infotheft: The increasingly frequent felony of peddling stolen intellectual property.

Infrastructure: A critical resource that cannot depend on improvised fixes.

Infrastructure Loss: What is missed when isolated solutions are no longer sufficient to do the job.

Innovation: Understanding when customers are ready to accept something new.

Integrated **D**efense **I**nformation **S**ystem: Any one from many choices that do not connect to each other.

Justification of Computers: Tolerating enthusiasm instead of economics.

Keyboard Phobia: An affliction that will keep much of the population from using computers.

Knowledge: Brains that leave the workplace every night and may not return.

Legacy Software: Old procedures perpetuated on new processors.

Legal System: Substituting public litigation for private morality.

Local Area Network: Costly efforts by enthusiastic amateurs seeking intellectual challenge, improved resumes, and indispensability.

© 1995 by The Information Economics Press

Luck: Delivering what pleases management in the absence of any guidance.

Macintosh: Name of a fruit. Redrawn by many from an original that was a copy.

Mainframe Computing: Centralized information services that are universally disliked, especially by those who want their own centralized information services.

Management: People who reach positions of power by recognizing only gains, but not any losses.

Methodology: A simple procedure that I understand and like because I can control it.

Microcomputer: A device that is like a puppy: buying one is easier than feeding it, grooming it, paying for sick calls, and cleaning up the mess when it fails to function properly.

Microsoft: Proof that the skill at poker is a prerequisite for success in the computer industry.

Military Information Systems: Devices purchased to satisfy the need at the beginning of a very long acquisition cycle.

Misinformation: Sophisticated analysis to improve flawed data.

Multimedia: Telephone, computer, publishing, cable, television, movie, and radio companies making claims against each other's franchises. A game of grabbing assets that eventually may have little value.

Multimedia **Interface:** Spectacular software that uses color, motion, and sound to mask a lack of substance.

Network Control: A simple solution to a problem that is usually tackled poorly by enthusiastic amateurs.

Obsolescence: Something that occurs when hardware becomes useless faster than the knowledge to use it.

Open **Systems:** A scheme to extend the economic life of information technologies.

Opinion Survey: A reflection of what someone wishes others to believe. The preferred choice of consultants and magazines because it does not cost much.

Over-Inspired Leadership: A managerial style that innovates regardless of what the followers may wish to do.

Paperless Office: Something that will happen when people start communicating by telepathy.

Paperwork Factory: Systems design by manufacturing engineers who found jobs in banking and insurance.

Password: A means for protecting sensitive information, about as effective as a fishnet umbrella.

People as Peripherals: Design that requires people to adjust to computers.

Pentagon: Where four military services are learning how to fight jointly enemies that already have a unified command.

Personal **Computer:** A device which is more responsive than the boss, co-workers, and some members of the family, and therefore loved with possessive passion.

Planning: The capacity to anticipate what to do while keeping in mind what to avoid.

Policy: The latest declaration from the chief executive that negates prior declarations.

Polls: Opinions of people eager to say what you wish to hear.

Privacy of Information: Only feasible is on a deserted island. Even then, caution is advisable.

Procedural Programming: Illogical means for the specially initiated to communicate with a device that supposedly process logic.

Process **Model:** An analyst's understanding of reality.

Process Redesign: Eliminating employees who should not have been employed to begin with. A method for disguising executive misjudgment for past hiring practices.

Prototyping: Testing the feasibility of doing a project with only a fraction of the required investment.

Quality: Something that can be judged only by paying customers, not by experts.

Reengineering: A widely advertised remedy for corporate ills, available in a variety of packages.

Reincarnation: A theological concept that calls for infinitely reusable software. Fervent faith is required for implementation.

© 1995 by The Information Economics Press

Reinventing Government: Similar to an attempt to improve the marketability of vinegar by changing the label.

Research on the Benefits of Computers: Opinion surveys with statistics.

Responsibility: Making clear what are the roles of the leaders and the followers.

Risk: Something that is never fully disclosed when asking for a computer budget.

Security Organization: Figuring out who will watch the watchers.

Simulated Decisions: Proving the expected results by programming the answers.

III

Simulation: A technique to imitate the real thing that often becomes confused with the real thing.

Software - **As Described to Management:** An idea that might work someday. An explanation to get the project funded.

Software - **When Announced to Customers:** A widely advertised promotion for the sole purpose of preempting competitive offerings.

Software - **When First Made Available:** Software where the customer pays for the privilege of completing whatever the developer forgot to finish.

Software - **Third Release:** The customer pays again for the first version of software that works, although not as originally promised.

Software: Primarily a social process involving people who have great difficulty in agreeing to what they want.

Software Agents: Endowing messages with sufficient intelligence to negotiate their way past useless bureaucracies.

Soviet Style Computing: Where the individual worker has no options in making decisions. Widely imitated in government agencies.

Stages of Growth Theory: Helping CIOs justify steadily rising computing budgets while profits decline. The basis for many consulting practices.

Standardization: Choosing one of the many standards on which to bet your company's money.

Stealth Computer Expenses: The cost of financial analysts, administrators, and secretaries doing work previously done by computer specialists. A trick to cut the officially reported computer budget.

Strategic Investment: A phrase always used to explain spending that has no payoff.

Strategy: Any proposal to get money for a journey to an unknown but glorious destination without mentioning the perils. A prerequisite for computer budgeting.

Systems Analysis: A thorough examination of technology to avoid questions about other causes.

Systems Failure: An explanation to divert the anger of customers from incompetent suppliers.

Systems Framework: A technological concept conceived without regard to business reality.

Systems Paralysis Cycle: The time left to do productive work after indoctrination, fact-finding, budget negotiation, and planning for the next promotion.

Systems **Planning:** The search for an instant fix to chronic problems. Repeated during each budget review.

Systems Specifications: An attempt at communication among tribes that do not share the same language, values, priorities or religion. These tribes are commonly known as management, users, analysts, programmers, and computer operators.

Teamwork: Figuring out how to get work done with someone who does not completely fit.

Technology Progress: Something measured by the amount of discarded computing equipment.

Terrorist Systems: The free enterprise solution to equipping terrorists with the latest technologies, purchased at attractive prices, and available for an immediate attack.

Tooth-to-Tail Ratio: The ratio of fighters to administrators plus consultants.

© 1995 by The Information Economics Press

Training: Time expended learning why the computer did not follow the instructions that the employee was taught to use.

UNIX: A means for inhibiting the understanding how to use computers.

User **Requirements:** Ordering a well-fitting suit without revealing most of the body to be clothed.

Virtual Reality: A refuge for those who dislike reality.

Vision: Prescribing how a business ought to operate on the basis of somebody else's practices. Requires no fact-gathering.

Visionary: Someone who asks you to climb a ladder that leads to an unexplored destination. Usually proposed by someone who has never been on a ladder before.

Wide Area Networks: A pathway for professional infocriminals to attack local networks guarded by amateurs.

Xerox: A copy corporation that start-up ventures love to copy. It contributed to the advancement of the U.S. information industry by making duplication easy.

Recent Dictionary Entries

Architecture of Information: Dividing the sphere of influence among contending factions.

Client/Server: A data center of their own for those dissatisfied with anyone else's data center. Previously used to describe mankind's oldest profession, which explains its current popularity.

Critical Success Factors: Consensus about causes of failure by those who caused the failure.

High Performance Computing: The answer is teraflops, but the question is uncertain.

Information Resource Management: Entrusting general management responsibilities to a specialist.

Justification of Computers: Not analytically feasible without cheating. Only more productive people can be justified.

Long Range Systems Planning: A three-ring binder containing recommendations as to when to upgrade computers and software.

Market Share: The most trustworthy opinion poll, since customers voted with their checkbooks.

Migration Systems: An application of Darwin's theory of survival-of-the-fittest to information management.

Object-Oriented Design: Semi-replicable method for transforming alchemy and witchcraft into experimental science.

Object-Oriented Programming: Components that may help transform software from a handcraft to a manufactured product, someday.

Outsourcing: Leaving torn and dirty underwear with a laundry and expecting new clothing in return.

Personal Data Assistant: Advanced technology of no particular use. Performance improves dramatically every month without affecting usefulness.

Privacy: A privilege to use company computers to produce resumes, holiday mailing lists, and alibi memos.

Return-on-Assets: An assumption that land, buildings, and machines explain profitability. Used in calculating management bonuses.

Return-on-Management: An assumption that the effectiveness of management explains profitability. Never used in calculating management bonuses.

Soviet Union: An organization with one of the worst information management records in history. Based on secrecy, misinformation and central control. Widely imitated under a different label.

Standards: Consent imposed by those who already dominate the market.

User Interface: Software that substitutes form for substance.

A free supply of *Irreverent Dictionaries* will be supplied to anyone proposing a new dictionary entry. Please submit your ideas to:

The Information Economics Press
POB 264
New Canaan, CT., 06840
or, by fax to 203-966-5506

Quotations from the Politics of Information Management

- Computerization is the conduct of management by other means.
- Policy is what you do, not what you say or write.
- Control of the sources of information is the essence of all managerial power.
- Only people can be productive, not computers.
- Politics is the art of getting and retaining power.
- Policy is to management what law is to governance.
- It is the balance of power, not centralization or decentralization, that matters.
- An exclusively technical solution is form without substance.
- Complex organizations require complex governance.
- A constitution is policy that endures over changes in management.
- Without verifiable results management promises are only desires.
- Government that governs the least will survive the longest.
- The proof of a workable system is found in everyday conduct.
- Standards are a compromise between chaos and stagnation.
- There is no quick long term fix.
- The faster we go the closer we have to examine the signs that guide us.
- The strange may be understood better through the familiar.
- The future is always built on what has happened before.
- Personal privacy is the foundation of all freedom.

- Without security all other privileges lapse.
- You cannot reengineer something that was not engineered to begin with.
- If you do what you have always done, you will get what you always got.
- Software is a new form of immortality.
- Wealth grows from a steady accumulation of useful knowledge.
- The capacity to learn is the basis for all future gains.
- Tools are a measure of all human progress.
- Ill-defined directions lead to confused implementation.
- Without purpose doing anything well is a waste.
- Uncertain leaders have perplexed followers.
- Sound directions will make even mediocrity look better.
- Every long-term plan starts with today's actions.
- There are more useful lessons in understanding mistakes than in analyzing successes.
- Listen to your enemies. They are the only ones who will tell you everything you did wrong.
- Hardship is one of the prerequisites for all advancement.
- Progress is the addition of what is new to what already works.
- Conflicting directions lead to hesitant action.
- If it looks too good, you may have incomplete information.
- Fear comes from the unknown, though much of what is yet to come is already here.
- The present is only the pre-history of an information-based civilization.
- Information politics must take precedence over information technology.

Order from The Information Economics press:

Paul A. Strassmann, *Information Payoff - The Transformation of Work in the Electronic Age*, The Free Press, 1985, 298 pages, 22 illustrations. Price: $35.95 (ISBN 0-02-931720-7)

Paul A. Strassmann, *The Business Value of Computers - An Executive's Guide*, The Information Economics Press, 1990, 548 pages, 184 illustrations. Price: $49.00 (ISBN 0-9620413-2-7)

John V. Titsworth, *Win Some, Lose Some - My 40 Years in Corporate America*, The Information Economics Press, 1992, 209 pages, 17 illustrations. Price: $14.95 (ISBN 0-9620413-3-5)

Paul A. Strassmann, *The Politics of Information Management - Policy Guidelines*, The Information Economics Press, 1995, 554 pages, 91 illustrations. Price: $49.00 (ISBN 0-9620413-4-3

Paul A. Strassmann and John Klossner, *Irreverent Dictionary of Information Politics*, The Information Economics Press, 1995, 152 pages, 141 illustrations. Price: $14.95 (ISBN 0-9620413-5-1)

TELEPHONE ORDERS: 800-800-0448; FAX ORDERS: 203-966-5506.
AMEX, VISA AND MASTERCARD ACCEPTED. SHIPPING COSTS ADDED.